Bringing Lent Home with

Saint Thérèse of Lisieux

Prayers, Reflections, and
Activities for Families

Donna-Marie Cooper O'Boyle

ave maria press AmP notre dame, indiana

Excerpts from *Story of a Soul*, translated by John Clarke, O.C.D., Copyright © 1975, 1976, 1996 by Washington Province of Discalced Carmelites, are used by permission of ICS Publications, 2131 Lincoln Road, NE, Washington, DC 20002-1199, USA www.icspublications.org.

Founded in 1865, Ave Maria Press is a ministry of the United States Province of Holy Cross.

www.avemariapress.com

Paperback: ISBN-10 1-59471-421-5, ISBN-13 978-1-59471-421-4

E-book ISBN-10 1-59471-466-5, 1SBN-13 978-1-59471-466-5

Cover image © *Art Archive, The*/SuperStock.

Cover and text design by Katherine Robinson.

Printed and bound in the United States of America.

Lovingly, for my children:

Justin,

Chaldea,

Jessica,

Joseph,

and

Mary-Catherine

ACKNOWLEDGMENTS

With a grateful heart to my family and friends, especially my parents, Eugene Joseph and Alexandra Mary Cooper; and my brothers and sisters, Alice Jean, Gene, Gary, Barbara, Tim, Michael, and David, I am eternally indebted. I am deeply grateful to Saint Thérèse of Lisieux for her inspiration and guidance in my life and especially as I wrote this book.

My children—Justin, Chaldea, Jessica, Joseph, and Mary-Catherine—I love you! My husband, David, the wind beneath my wings, thank you for your love and support!

Special thanks to Robert Hamma, Thomas Grady, and the wonderfully diligent team at Ave Maria Press for their partnership in getting this book out to you!

INTRODUCTION

The Church offers the faithful a marvelous opportunity for spiritual growth and conversion during the penitential season of Lent. With God's grace and our faithful efforts in prayer, fasting, and almsgiving, we can make the most of this time of year to grow deeper in holiness and please God, all the while growing closer as a family.

In his final homily on Ash Wednesday of 2013, Pope Benedict XVI invited us to turn wholeheartedly to God during Lent:

> The Church proposes to us, first, the strong appeal that the prophet Joel addressed to the people of Israel, "Thus says the Lord, return to me with all your heart, with fasting, with weeping, and with mourning" (2:12). Please note the phrase "with all your heart," which means from the center of our thoughts and feelings, from the roots of our decisions, choices and actions, with a gesture of total and radical freedom. But is this return to God possible? Yes, because there is a force that does not reside in our hearts, but that emanates from the heart of God. It is the power of his mercy. The prophet says, further: "Return to the Lord your God, for he is gracious and merciful, slow to anger, rich in faithful love, ready to repent of evil" (v. 13). The return to the Lord is possible as "grace," because it is the work of God and the fruit of that faith that we place in His mercy.[1]

Called to be first and foremost educators, Christian parents can help mold their children's consciences and souls immensely by offering a continual example of charity and forgiveness, practicing the virtues, and creating a loving atmosphere of family prayer in their home—their domestic church.

Saint Thérèse of Lisieux is an outstanding spiritual guide for our family Lenten journey. Her teachings are simple enough for children to grasp, yet her unique understanding of what is necessary to grow in holiness is extensive.

During a season that is meant to transform hearts and souls, this book will provide and encourage a daily occurrence of family prayer and communication as you journey through Lent together. By following the suggestions regarding how your family can apply Saint Thérèse's wisdom to your lives, you will participate more fully with the rhythm of the Church regarding Lenten prayer, fasting, and almsgiving.

You can choose morning or evening (or hopefully both) to gather with your brood. Your time will be well spent reflecting on Saint Thérèse of Lisieux's life and insight as well as the great traditions of Holy Mother Church.

To use this book, simply gather your family and move page by page, day by day, forging your way through Lent. You can come together morning or evening at your kitchen table, around a prayer table, or wherever you feel most comfortable when praying as a family in your domestic church. Make it special—light a prayer candle if you wish.

Saint Thérèse's Inspiration: Each day a quote from Saint Thérèse begins the page and sets the tone, in a sense, for the Lenten day.

Parent Reflection: You will be given points to ponder in this section each day. Some of it will be for you and some for your children.

Family Prayer: There are two opportunities for prayer during each day of meditations—one at the beginning and one at the end. Feel free to elaborate and adapt to suit your family's needs.

A Story from Saint Thérèse's Life: This book as a whole will tell the story of Saint Thérèse's life from the earliest years, high-lighting notable parts. This section can be read by an older child or a parent.

Fasting: Each day, "fasting" suggestions will be made to help guide you (the parent) and your children about what to fast from. It will not only be from certain foods, but more often it will be fasting from bad habits or enjoyable activities. Feel free to adapt it to what works best for your family.

Ash Wednesday and Good Friday are days of fasting and absti-nence. Church law requires that no meat may be eaten on these days by Catholics fourteen years old and older. People with medical conditions and pregnant or nursing mothers are exempt from fasting and abstinence. Catholics from the age of eighteen through fifty-nine must fast on these days having one full meatless meal and two smaller meatless and penitential meals. The two small meals together should not equal a full meal.

Almsgiving: Each day "almsgiving" suggestions are provided to help with ideas to accomplish as a family or individually.

Prayer: Each day you will be given a simple yet poignant thought to think and pray about throughout the day.

You will see that there are no entries for Saturdays of Lent. I suggest that you use the Sunday prayers and activities throughout the weekend. The suggestions for almsgiving on Sundays may take a little longer to do and are appropriate for the weekend when there is more time.

Saint Thérèse of Lisieux wrote a beautiful morning prayer that expresses how each day of our lives should be a prayer offered from a heart in love with God. Pray this prayer each morning throughout Lent and beyond as well.

> O my God! I offer thee all my actions of this day for the intentions and for the glory of the Sacred Heart of Jesus. I desire to sanctify every beat of my heart, my every thought, my simplest works, by uniting them to Its infinite merits; and I wish to make reparation for my sins by casting them into the furnace of Its Merciful Love. O my God! I ask of thee for myself and for those whom I hold dear, the grace to fulfill perfectly thy Holy Will, to accept for love of thee the joys and sorrows of this passing life, so that we may one day be united together in heaven for all Eternity. Amen.

May your family receive rich blessings as you all journey closer to heaven and its rewards through this Lenten season.

ASH WEDNESDAY

You know well enough that our Lord does not look so much at the greatness of our actions, nor even at their difficulty, but at the love with which we do them.

—*Story of a Soul*

Parent Reflection

As we begin Lent, we are called to deepen our prayer life. In so doing, we—in a sense—enlarge our hearts with love for God and our fellow human beings. Today when you gather your family, explain to the children that we try to do three things each day during Lent. First, we give up something. This is called fasting. Second, we give something to others—help, possessions, or money we share with others. This is called almsgiving. Finally, we pray more. All three of these things should be part of our daily lives, but Lent is a season for doing them more intensely.

You may want to ask the children if they have decided to *give up* something for Lent or if they have chosen to *do something* special to please Jesus. Take a few moments to help them formulate their Lenten resolutions. These should be simple actions that they can accomplish throughout the season. You can share with them what you are planning to do this Lent as well. Have the children (with your help) write down their resolutions to be used as a reminder to them of what they have committed to do this Lenten season. They can hang their Lenten resolutions on their bedroom door, put them on a prayer table, or keep them in their pockets or backpacks.

Saint Thérèse's words above remind us that God isn't expecting perfection from us. Sure, he wants us to try hard and strive to do our tasks as well as we are able, but it's not a competition! Rather, our good Lord is very pleased with the love we put into our faithful actions.

Family Prayer

All make the Sign of the Cross.

Parent: Dear Jesus, help us to be faithful to our Lenten resolutions. Guide us to have a better understanding of Ash Wednesday and the penitential season that we begin today. Please grant us the graces we need to travel through this holy season with faith, hope, and love. Now let us listen to these words of Saint Thérèse.

A parent or child reads the opening quotation aloud.

All: Blessed Mother Mary, be with us as we gather to pray on this Ash Wednesday, beginning our Lenten journey.

Saint Thérèse, please pray for us. Amen.

A Story from Saint Thérèse's Life

Saint Thérèse, the youngest of nine children, was born in Alençon, France, on January 2, 1873, as Marie-Françoise-Thérèse Martin. Her father, Louis, who had once dreamed of being a monk, became a husband and father instead and made his living as a successful jeweler and watchmaker. Thérèse's mother, Zélie Guerin, had considered becoming a religious to serve God and the sick, but God had other plans for Zélie. Instead, she cared for her children and husband and also kept her hands quite busy creating lace; she immersed herself in that trade when she was discouraged from becoming a nun.

The close-knit Martin family endured much sorrow. Four of Thérèse's siblings died of enteritis at a young age: three as infants and one at five-and-a-half years old. The family might have seemed ordinary otherwise, but the remaining five girls were all inspired to enter religious life, which indicates a pretty extraordinary, faith-filled family open to God's graces. Four of the daughters became contemplative Carmelites at Lisieux Carmel, and the other became a Visitation sister.

Fasting

Discuss with your children what you can offer to God as a sacrifice during Lent. Can you and the kids give up a dessert, a TV show, a video game, or the Internet at times? Decide what you will all do as a family. Encourage the children to do something individually.

Almsgiving

In Saint Thérèse's simple words of wisdom featured at the start of todays's meditation, we learn that the Lord is looking for our love (not things). List three ways your family can show love to others outside the immediate family—a neighbor, a friend, or a relative.

Prayer

Today's Intention: Let's pray to try to do everything with love.

Closing Prayer: Dear Jesus, thank you for loving me! Saint Thérèse loved with all her heart. Teach me to open my heart fully to your love and to be more generous.

All pray the Our Father, Hail Mary, and Glory Be.

All through the Day: Jesus will teach me to love.

The little bird sings all the time.
His life doesn't worry him.
One grain of seed makes him happy.
He never sows here below.
—*The Poetry of Saint Thérèse of Lisieux*

Parent Reflection

Is it possible to stop worrying completely? Perhaps this is an extra challenging feat for parents whose job is to be responsible for their offspring. Yet, our Lord would like us to try to offer up all our worries and to trust him with our lives. Saint Thérèse expresses this sentiment in her verse about a little bird. Let today be a day of trust and surrender.

Family Prayer

All make the Sign of the Cross.

Parent: Dear Jesus, please visit us here in our home. Help us to open our hearts to the graces you wish to give us today. Now let us listen to these words of Saint Thérèse.

A parent or child reads the opening quotation aloud.

All: Blessed Mother Mary, bring us closer to your Son, Jesus.

Saint Thérèse, please pray for us. Amen.

A Story from Saint Thérèse's Life

Soon after Saint Thérèse was born, the same illness that had stolen away her siblings threatened her as well. Upon the doctor's advice, she was sent to live in the forests of Bocage at Semalle with Rose Taille as her wet nurse. There she dwelled, away from the illness, faring well as a peasant baby. She returned to her doting family when she was fifteen months old.

Thérèse's parents showered her with affection and educated her and her sisters in a thoroughly Catholic domestic church with much emphasis on family prayer, practicing the virtues, visiting the sick, and attending daily Mass. Though Thérèse felt passionately called at a young age to seek holiness and become a nun, she grew up as a regular girl and possessed a rather sensitive nature. She was at times spoiled, stomping her feet and throwing temper tantrums, but at other times, she played angelically and pretended to be a nun.

Fasting

Even seemingly small sacrifices are very meaningful when done with great love. Can you and the children give up a special treat today—something you really enjoy?

Almsgiving

Create a greeting card with the kids and include a comforting message, even one as simple as "Jesus loves you!" Mail the card or drop it off in someone's mailbox.

Prayer

Today's Intention: Let's pray to hear the inspiration of the Holy Spirit speaking to our hearts.

Closing Prayer: Dear Jesus, thank you for our family. Please help us to love one another, putting one another before ourselves.

All pray the Our Father, Hail Mary, and Glory Be.

All through the Day: I will trust God like a little bird would!

I understood how all the flowers He has created are beautiful, how the splendor of the rose and the whiteness of the lily do not take away from the perfume of the little violet or the delightful simplicity of the daisy. I understood that if all flowers wanted to be roses, nature would lose her springtime beauty, and the fields would no longer be decked out with little wild flowers.

—*Story of a Soul*

Parent Reflection

Each one of our children possesses his or her own distinctive gifts to share with the family and the world. At times, we may shake our heads in amazement, observing their vast differences in temperaments and behaviors. Seize the moment to teach your kids that we are all given unique gifts we can use to help others. No one person is better than another. We need both roses and wild flowers!

Family Prayer

All make the Sign of the Cross.

Parent: Dear Jesus, help us to respect one another's differences. Teach us to use our own gifts to aid one another. Now let us listen to these words of Saint Thérèse.

A parent or child now reads aloud the opening quotation.

All: Blessed Mother Mary, bring us closer to your Son, Jesus.

Saint Thérèse, please pray for us. Amen.

A Story from Saint Thérèse's Life

Thérèse was strong willed as a child and was known to be mischievous, but she was a happy little girl and brought an abundance of joy into the Martin household. Perhaps it was Thérèse's strong spirit that helped her persevere and decide to cross the threshold of the convent to become a nun a few years later despite great difficulties in doing so. Thérèse had much to overcome in her short life, including the loss of her mother when she was only four-and-a-half years old. Zélie died of breast cancer at the age of forty-five. In her last days, Zélie prepared her daughters Pauline and Marie to help raise Thérèse, telling them she wouldn't be a problem—she was a "chosen spirit."

Fasting

Today, fast from grumbling. Tell the kids that if they are tempted to be negative in any way, they should stop and say this prayer: "Help me, Jesus."

Almsgiving

Give some time away today. We are all busy, but take a moment to compliment a family member or help someone with a chore. If possible, take this loving act out beyond the household too.

Prayer

> *Today's Intention*: Let's pray to be more attentive to those in need, especially those in our own home.
>
> *Closing Prayer*: Dear Jesus, help me to respect others' differences and give of myself to make someone happier.
>
> *All pray the Our Father, Hail Mary, and Glory Be.*
>
> *All through the Day*: God gives me special and unique gifts to share.

FIRST SUNDAY OF LENT

O my Beloved, how gentle and humble of heart You seem under the veil of the white Host! To teach me humility, you cannot humble yourself further. Therefore, to respond to your love, I desire that my sisters always put me in the lowest place and I want to convince myself that this place is indeed mine.

—The Prayers of Saint Thérèse of Lisieux

Parent Reflection

Today is the first Sunday of Lent. All of the gospels for the Church's three-year cycle of readings (Mt 4:1–11; Mk 1:12–15; Lk 4:1–13) focus on Jesus' temptation by the devil in the desert. The devil, as we know, sought to persuade Jesus to bow down and worship him. Of course, the humble Jesus did not fall for any of the devil's deception.

Saint Thérèse earnestly tried to live humbly. She could easily have given in and allowed the devil to tempt her to be prideful. Each morning, Saint Thérèse began her day resolving to be humble, and she continually asked God to help her. Each evening, she asked for forgiveness for any time she didn't cooperate with God's grace. Faithfulness to prayer gave Saint Thérèse strength and hope.

We often seek a higher place. Saint Thérèse sought the lowest place in desiring to be more like Jesus and to please him. We can also pray like Saint Thérèse to prevent falling into discouragement when things go wrong and to remain humble of heart.

Family Prayer

All make the Sign of the Cross.

Parent: Dear Jesus, help us to become humble like you. Now let us listen to these words of Saint Thérèse.

A parent or child reads the opening quotation aloud.

All: Blessed Mother Mary, bring us closer to your Son, Jesus.

Saint Thérèse, please pray for us. Amen.

A Story from Saint Thérèse's Life

At the age of four, Thérèse watched her father cry and was utterly crushed as she knelt by her mother's bed and saw Zélie receiving the last sacraments. Later in life, Thérèse would write, "When Mummy died, my happy disposition changed."[2] She was young, sensitive, and impressionable and carried every bit of the memory of her suffering mother in her heart.

"Every detail of my mother's illness is still with me, especially her last weeks on earth."[3] After her mother's death, Thérèse found comfort with her family, but she was often weepy and oversensitive around others.

Fasting

Today, fast from falling into temptations to be prideful. If you or your children feel the urge to boast, pause and consider a way to draw attention to someone else's accomplishments.

Almsgiving

Give away a higher place today. If you'd like to have first choice of a television show, game, or kind of treat to eat, give the choice to someone else instead.

Prayer

Today's Intention: Let's pray today for all those who have no choices in life, who may be oppressed in some way.

Closing Prayer: Dear Jesus, help us to come closer to you and learn from your holy humility.

All pray the Our Father, Hail Mary, and Glory Be.

All through the Day: I want to be more like Jesus and will try my very best to do so.

O my God, behold us as we bow before You. We can beseech You for the graces of working for Your Glory. . . . O my God! Grant us the grace to be more vigilant in seeking sacrifices than those who do not love you are in pursuit of worldly goods.

—*The Prayers of Saint Thérèse of Lisieux*

Parent Reflection

Whenever we pray, we in essence bow before God—that is, if our hearts are in the right place. Then our hearts can bow down before God no matter where we are, and our Lord will hear our prayers. Saint Thérèse's words above illustrate a faithful woman's desire to bow before God by seeking sacrifices to make up for those who are so preoccupied with the things of this world that they ignore God. Ponder a sacrifice you can put into practice today to please God.

Family Prayer

All make the Sign of the Cross.

> *Parent:* Dear Jesus, help our family to turn to you in every need. Urge us to seek sacrifices for the good of others and to please you. Now let us listen to these words of Saint Thérèse.

A parent or child reads the opening quotation aloud.

> *All:* Blessed Mother Mary, bring us closer to your Son, Jesus.

> Saint Thérèse, please pray for us. Amen.

A Story from Saint Thérèse's Life

Shortly after Thérèse's mother died, Thérèse's father decided to move his family from Alençon (the familiar place of his youth and marriage) to Lisieux in the Calvados Department of Normandy, where Zélie's brother, Isador Guerin, and his family lived. The comfort of being near relatives eased their transition. The Martin family settled into a spacious country home, *Les Buissonnets*. Thérèse's older sister Pauline then assumed the role of mother figure for Thérèse, who naturally grew very close to her sister.

Fasting

Today, fast from controversy and arguing. Yes, it's all around us, but let's choose to not get ensnared in it. Instead, offer a prayer for the situation.

Almsgiving

Today, give ten or fifteen minutes of time that you hoped to spend doing something you like. Give that time to someone else by calling them up, helping them with a task, or talking about an interest of theirs.

Prayer

Today's Intention: Let's pray for those who are ignored in some way or who might feel alone.

Closing Prayer: Dear Jesus, help our family to be more like Saint Thérèse, wanting to do small things with great love to please you.

All pray the Our Father, Hail Mary, and Glory Be.

All through the Day: I will bow before God in prayer through my thoughts and actions.

TUESDAY, FIRST WEEK OF LENT

See, then, all that Jesus lays claim to from us; He has no need of our works but only of our love, for the same God who declares He has no need to tell us when He is hungry did not fear to beg for a little water from the Samaritan woman. He was thirsty. But when He said, "Give me to drink," it was love of His poor creatures the Creator of the universe was seeking. He was thirsty for love.

—*Story of a Soul*

Parent Reflection

Jesus thirsts for our love. We can love him in so many ways. Even being faithful to our daily duties and doing everything with a loving heart shows God our love. He is the one who placed us in our families. He wants us to take care of our children to the best of our abilities. Ponder Jesus' thirst for your love today. Stress the need to love God with your children. How can you all give him a "drink"?

Family Prayer

All make the Sign of the Cross.

> *Parent*: Dear Jesus, help us to live our lives in loving, faithful service to you. Now let us listen to these words of Saint Thérèse.

A parent or child reads the opening quotation aloud.

> *All*: Blessed Mother Mary, bring us closer to your Son, Jesus.

> Saint Thérèse, please pray for us. Amen.

A Story from Saint Thérèse's Life

Saint Thérèse said that moving into *Les Buissonnets* in Normandy when she was four-and-a-half years old initiated the "second period" of her life, which lasted until she was fourteen. She said it was the most painful of the three parts of her life, and in it, she "entered into the serious side of life." Thérèse was taught at home by her sisters Marie and Pauline until she was eight-and-a-half years old. She then began school at the Abbey of Notre Dame du Pre in Lisieux, where she was taught by the Benedictine nuns. Thérèse excelled in her classes because she was taught so well at home, but because she showed such excellence at her tender age, others bullied her.

Fasting

Today, fast from negativity. Look at the bright side instead. If you are tempted to grumble or mope, say a prayer and hang on to hope instead of dwelling on the negative.

Almsgiving

Think of someone who might feel bullied. Ponder what you can do to help that person.

Prayer

Today's Intention: Let's pray for all those who are bullied or mistreated in some way.

Closing Prayer: Dear Jesus, please shine through us so that your love will comfort those around us who are in need. Show us ways to offer your love.

All pray the Our Father, Hail Mary, and Glory Be.

All through the Day: I want to be more aware of those who need my help.

Jesus is parched, for He meets only the ungrateful and indifferent among His disciples in the world, and among His own disciples, alas, He finds few hearts who surrender to Him without reservations, who understand the real tenderness of His infinite love.

—Story of a Soul

Parent Reflection

Do we ever really and truly appreciate God and his infinite love for us? Saint Thérèse lamented that we do not surrender our hearts fully to him. We get too busy to ponder his love for us—perhaps we're afraid, and many times we're ungrateful. Take some time today to tell your children about God's beautiful love. Think of ways to express it to them at their various levels of comprehension. Through your prayers today, ask God to remind you of his infinite love.

Family Prayer

All make the Sign of the Cross.

Parent: Dear Jesus, so often we are preoccupied with numerous things and give you very little time. Forgive our ungratefulness. We love you. Now let us listen to these words of Saint Thérèse.

A parent or child reads the opening quotation aloud.

All: Blessed Mother Mary, bring us closer to your Son, Jesus.

Saint Thérèse, please pray for us. Amen.

A Story from Saint Thérèse's Life

As a young girl, Thérèse had a difficult time at school because she was bullied. As a result, she felt overly sensitive and very inferior. She often would hide to avoid any sort of confrontation or attention given to her, sometimes crying in silence. Thérèse said that her five school years were the "saddest of my life" (*Story of a Soul*, 53). She felt she could survive the experience only because her sister Celine was there with her. Thérèse enjoyed telling stories to the younger children and looking after the infants.

Fasting

Today, fast from speaking ill of anyone, even if it is justified. Try your best to say a prayer for the person or situation instead.

Almsgiving

Today, make a special effort to cheer up someone who is feeling down. Smile and offer a compliment.

Prayer

> *Today's Intention*: Let us pray for all those who are misunderstood and those who are frightened.
>
> *Closing Prayer*: Dear Jesus, help us to be more sensitive to the needs of others during this Lenten season.
>
> *All pray the Our Father, Hail Mary, and Glory Be.*
>
> *All through the Day*: I will pray to understand the real tenderness of God's infinite love.

I am only a child, powerless and weak, and yet it is my weakness that gives me the boldness of offering myself as victim of Your Love, O Jesus!

—Story of a Soul

Parent Reflection

We have to admit that we have no valid excuses for not surrendering to God. Saint Thérèse emphasizes that it is in her weakness that she can become strong, brave, and bold enough to offer herself to Jesus. No matter what our personal circumstances may be, our Lord is calling us to surrender our hearts to him, even in our weakness. As parents, we can impress this upon our children too. They are never too young to learn to pray. Your example of praying with them during all situations sends a clear, resounding message to their hearts.

Family Prayer

All make the Sign of the Cross.

Parent: Dear Jesus, remind us that we should have childlike hearts when we come to you in prayer and that we should come to you often. Now let us listen to these words of Saint Thérèse.

A parent or child reads the opening quotation aloud.

All: Blessed Mother Mary, bring us closer to your Son, Jesus.

Saint Thérèse, please pray for us. Amen.

A Story from Saint Thérèse's Life

Little Thérèse enjoyed playing with her younger cousin, Marie Guerin. She thoroughly enjoyed visits to the park to play with her cousins and siblings and gather pretty flowers. Evenings were especially heartfelt to Thérèse. As soon as she came through the door after enduring the challenges of school, she climbed on her father's lap, and all of her worries and sadness melted in his warm, fatherly embrace.

Fasting

Today, fast from procrastination. If there's something you need to do, do it in a timely fashion and in a way pleasing to God (rather than haphazardly).

Almsgiving

Give away your worries. If something is bothering you, give it to God in prayer. Speak to your family about concerns or worries you may be enduring. While this may seem selfish rather than serving, you are actually serving one another (and God) by allowing them to help you.

Prayer

Today's Intention: Let's pray for peace in our world.

Closing Prayer: Dear Jesus, open our hearts to your great love for us.

All pray the Our Father, Hail Mary, and Glory Be.

All through the Day: God will give me the grace to be bold enough to surrender to him.

O, Jesus, I know it, love is repaid by love alone, and so I searched and I found the way to solace my heart by giving love for love.

—Story of a Soul

Parent Reflection

Saint Thérèse was all about love. Even as a young woman, she possessed the grace to understand the great mysteries of Christ's love. She has much to teach today's families about love. Her simple life of devotion can be an exemplary model for your family's life. Try your best to foster a loving atmosphere in your home today. Reward your children's good behavior with warm hugs.

Family Prayer

All make the Sign of the Cross.

Parent: Dear Jesus, teach our family your loving ways. Grant us the graces to desire to spread your love rather than seek our own comforts. Now let us listen to these words of Saint Thérèse.

A parent or child reads the opening quotation aloud.

All: Blessed Mother Mary, bring us closer to your Son, Jesus.

Saint Thérèse, please pray for us. Amen.

A Story from Saint Thérèse's Life

Thérèse and her sister Celine were very close. When Celine was preparing to make her First Holy Communion, Thérèse heard her sister Pauline explain the importance of promising to change one's life after receiving the sacrament. Though Thérèse was four years from receiving her First Communion, she listened intently to Pauline preparing and teaching Celine and decided on the spot to prepare her own heart to receive Jesus. Thérèse believed she received great graces on Celine's

First Communion day and said it was one of the most beautiful days in her life.

Fasting

Today, fast from bitterness. If you are tempted to act or speak bitterly in any way, try your best to pause and pray these words instead: "Jesus, help me to be loving."

Almsgiving

Count your blessings today. Thérèse was keenly aware of the love and blessings in her family. Help the kids to see that many blessings surround them. Write them down.

Prayer

> *Today's Intention*: Let's pray for the homeless and for people who feel alone.
>
> *Closing Prayer*: Dear Jesus, help me to love with your love.
>
> *All pray the Our Father, Hail Mary, and Glory Be.*
>
> *All through the Day*: God gives us many opportunities to love.

SECOND SUNDAY OF LENT

I understood that Pauline was going to leave me to enter a convent. I understood, too, she would not wait for me and I was about to lose my second *Mother!* Ah! How can I express the anguish of my heart!

—Story of a Soul

Parent Reflection

Today is the Second Sunday of Lent. The gospels for the Church's three-year cycle of readings speak about the Transfiguration of Jesus (Mt 17:1–9; Mk 9:2–10; Lk 9:28–36). Jesus revealed his glory to Peter, James, and John after taking them high up on a mountain. Jesus' face was shining as the sun, and his clothes were a dazzling, pure white. A voice from a cloud said, "This is my beloved Son, with whom I am well pleased; listen to him" (Mt 17:5).

The disciples were so filled with fear that they fell to the ground. Jesus reassured them that all was well and told them to get up. He told them not to tell anyone what they had witnessed until after he rose from the dead. The incredible privilege of seeing Jesus this way and hearing God the Father gave Peter, James, and John much strength for their journey ahead.

Saint Thérèse experienced fear and uncertainty when she lost her mother and then when her sister Pauline (her second mother) was leaving for the convent, as well as many other times throughout her fairly short life. Thérèse was aware of these normal human feelings but chose to cling to God's promises to her. God asks the same of us. He wants us to turn to him in all of our needs and to trust him with our lives no matter how we feel. He will come through for us.

Family Prayer

All make the Sign of the Cross.

Parent: Dear Jesus, help us to trust in you. Now let us listen to these words of Saint Thérèse.

A parent or child reads the opening quotation aloud.

All: Blessed Mother Mary, bring us closer to your Son, Jesus.

Saint Thérèse, please pray for us. Amen.

A Story from Saint Thérèse's Life

Thérèse's older sister Pauline was like a second mother to her. When Thérèse overheard that Pauline would be leaving for the convent, she was deeply troubled; she couldn't fathom losing another mother. But when Pauline explained how life would be at the Carmelite convent, Thérèse fell in love with the idea of becoming a nun. She said that she was not trying to imitate Pauline but that she became keenly aware of a strong calling to enter religious life for the sake of Jesus alone.

Fasting

During the upcoming week, fast from noise. Does that sound crazy? Try it. Do all you can this week to foster a quiet, peaceful atmosphere at home. Try to stay away from technology—even if it's just for thirty minutes each day. Set a timer for the kids.

Almsgiving

Talk to the kids about reaching out to others this week. Encourage them to be good helpers in the household, doing their chores without complaining. Think of someone you know who may be enduring a challenging situation. Can your family members put your heads together to plan a nice surprise for that person sometime this week (a handmade card, an encouraging phone call or email, a special dessert)?

Prayer

Today's Intention: Let us pray for children all over the world, that they would have loving homes and come closer to God.

Closing Prayer: Dear Jesus, help us to spread your love and to be a shining example to others.

All pray the Our Father, Hail Mary, and Glory Be.

All through the Day: Jesus will give me strength for the journey.

I still see the spot where I received Pauline's last kiss. . . . The whole family was in tears. . . . My soul was flooded with sadness!

—*Story of a Soul*

Parent Reflection

A family is indeed a beautiful union of people whom God has destined to grow together. Where would we be without our family members? We grow in holiness in the hearts of our homes. Every happening—happy or sad, challenging or easy—can become a wonderful opportunity for grace. Focus today on the blessedness of your family. If the kids argue, calmly remind them they are to resolve their differences and love one another. If you experience difficulties today, pause and ask God to transform your heart and the trials into prayers united to his sufferings so that graces will be merited for your family. Try not to waste the opportunities for grace.

Family Prayer

All make the Sign of the Cross.

Parent: Dear Jesus, open our hearts to your graces. Now let us listen to these words of Saint Thérèse.

A parent or child reads the opening quotation aloud.

All: Blessed Mother Mary, bring us closer to your Son, Jesus.

Saint Thérèse, please pray for us. Amen.

A Story from Saint Thérèse's Life

Even though Thérèse experienced great difficulty accepting it when her sister Pauline left to enter the convent, Thérèse was very intrigued with the thought of entering the convent herself when she was older. Every Thursday, Thérèse and her family visited Pauline at Carmel. Before Pauline's entrance into Carmel, she and Thérèse were inseparable, so visiting Pauline once a week for a few minutes just wasn't enough for Thérèse. She fell ill.

Fasting

Today, fast from idle time. If you find your kids have nothing to do (or are spending too much time watching TV or surfing the Internet), urge everyone to do something worthwhile. Give the children direction. Suggest that they think of ways they can help someone, make a greeting card, or assist you with chores.

Almsgiving

Today, in addition to your prayers, give God at least thirty minutes of your time. That could be accomplished reading the lives of the saints or *The Catechism of the Catholic Church*, spending quiet time in contemplation, or doing a work of mercy for someone. If not today, try to do it soon.

Prayer

Today's Intention: Let's pray for broken families and families facing serious challenges.

Closing Prayer: Dear Jesus, thank you for the blessing of our family.

All pray the Our Father, Hail Mary, and Glory Be.

All through the Day: Our family is meant to grow together in holiness and love.

TUESDAY, SECOND WEEK OF LENT

My greatest consolation when I was sick was to receive a letter from Pauline . . . the thought of one day becoming a Carmelite [like Pauline] made me live.

—*Story of a Soul*

Parent Reflection

Being a Christian parent compels us to practice virtues in the household. A whole lot of compassion and forgiveness should be doled out as we raise our children. They are a work in progress after all. Caring for a family means caring not only for externals (food and shelter) but for the hearts and souls of the children who are entrusted to our care by God—an awesome responsibility. What can you do today to make your home a center of compassion and forgiveness?

Family Prayer

All make the Sign of the Cross.

> *Parent*: Dear Jesus, help us to care for the needs of our family, putting others first. Now let us listen to these words of Saint Thérèse.

A parent or child reads the opening quotation aloud.

> *All*: Blessed Mother Mary, bring us closer to your Son, Jesus.

Saint Thérèse, please pray for us. Amen.

A Story from Saint Thérèse's Life

A strange illness suddenly afflicted little Thérèse. She trembled uncontrollably, and the doctor was called to the house. The serious illness puzzled everyone because Thérèse was very young to have contracted it. The family surrounded Thérèse, doling out comfort and love throughout her suffering. Thérèse feared she was somehow making up the illness, but she was assured by the doctor and her confessor that she was not. Still her heart felt troubled. The illness deeply troubled Thérèse's father too, and he requested Masses be said at Our Lady of Victories in Paris for his "little queen."

Fasting

Encourage the children to fast from a treat today (a dessert, a snack, or a TV show).

Almsgiving

Talk to the children about offering help to a classmate, a sibling, or a parent. Talk to them about doing their chores without being asked.

Prayer

> *Today's Intention*: Let us pray for all those who are sick and suffering.
>
> *Closing Prayer*: Dear Jesus, help our family to be mindful of others who may be suffering in some way.
>
> *All pray the Our Father, Hail Mary, and Glory Be.*
>
> *All through the Day*: God wants me to enter more fully into a spirit of self-denial this Lenten season.

A miracle was necessary and it was Our Lady of Victories who worked it. . . . All of a sudden the Blessed Virgin appeared beautiful to me. . . . What penetrated to the depths of my soul was the ravishing smile of the Blessed Virgin. . . . All my pain disappeared.

—*Story of a Soul*

Parent Reflection

The Blessed Mother has much to teach us. She remained with her Son, Jesus, to the bitter end and witnessed every drop of blood he shed on our behalf. While in his agony on the Cross, Jesus gave his Mother, Mary, to all of us to be our Mother. While Mary won't always perform miracles for us as she did with Saint Thérèse the day she was cured of her illness, Mary will work miracles in our hearts and will indeed bring us closer to her Son. We need to ask her to guide us.

Family Prayer

All make the Sign of the Cross.

Parent: Dear Jesus, thank you for your Mother, Mary. Now let us listen to these words of Saint Thérèse.

A parent or child reads the opening quotation aloud.

All: Blessed Mother Mary, bring us closer to your Son, Jesus.

Saint Thérèse, please pray for us. Amen.

A Story from Saint Thérèse's Life

One day Thérèse's illness left her begging for her family to come quickly to help her. They desperately tried to console her, but Thérèse knew in her heart that she had to turn to the Blessed Mother for the heavenly help she urgently needed. Her sisters knelt by her bedside and prayed fervently. Thérèse also prayed with all her heart that the Mother of Heaven would take pity on her. Suddenly, Thérèse saw

Mary "so beautiful that never had I seen anything so attractive" (*Story of a Soul*, 65). Mary smiled at Thérèse, and instantly all of Thérèse's pain and suffering vanished. She was cured!

Fasting

Today, fast from fear. If anything is causing you to be fearful, say a prayer and give the fear to God. Ask the Blessed Mother to help you hand over your fears.

Almsgiving

Ask the children to choose a family member whom they will secretly pray for throughout today.

Prayer

Today's Intention: Let's pray for all those in seemingly impossible situations.

Closing Prayer: Dear Jesus, please help our family to draw closer to you today.

All pray the Our Father, Hail Mary, and Glory Be.

All through the Day: The Blessed Mother wants to mother us.

I did love reading much. . . . I had human *angels*, fortunately for me, to guide me in the choice of books which, while being entertaining, nourished both my heart and my mind. . . . Never did God permit me to read a single one that was capable of doing me any harm.

—*Story of a Soul*

Parent Reflection

Being a Catholic parent means you'll be thoroughly invested in your children's education. You actually help form their consciences with your parenting measures. Saint Thérèse was fortunate to have holy parents and influences in her life. I'm reminded of my friend Fr. Bill C. Smith (now deceased) who cautioned our congregation: "Don't put that garbage in your head!" He was referring to inappropriate movies and television programs, books and magazines that we should not engage in. We must be vigilant and oversee everything our children learn. Just because a movie is rated for ages thirteen and older does not mean it is appropriate for a teenager. What the world considers suitable and what a Christian parent does are two completely different things! Expose your children to wholesome Christian media and read the lives of the saints to them often.

Family Prayer

All make the Sign of the Cross.

> *Parent*: Dear Jesus, help us to always choose what is right and good. Now let us listen to these words of Saint Thérèse.

A parent or child reads the opening quotation aloud.

> *All*: Blessed Mother Mary, bring us closer to your Son, Jesus.

> Saint Thérèse, please pray for us. Amen.

A Story from Saint Thérèse's Life

Thérèse said that her joy in seeing the Blessed Mother smile at her was soon turned to sadness. Thérèse was very thankful to be cured and to have received grace in that holy experience, but after she shared it with others, she felt troubled. Many people questioned her, and Thérèse began to fear she had lied. She said, "The Blessed Virgin permitted this torment for my soul's good, as perhaps without it I would have had some thought of vanity" (*Story of a Soul*, 67).

Fasting

Today, fast from frowning. When something annoys or bothers you, practice smiling instead.

Almsgiving

Ask the children to think of three positive things they can do today to brighten someone's spirits. Help them write them down.

Prayer

> *Today's Intention*: Let's pray for the Church and all its members.
>
> *Closing Prayer*: Dear Jesus, help me to see every gift as coming from you. I can do nothing without you.
>
> *All pray the Our Father, Hail Mary, and Glory Be.*
>
> *All through the Day*: I should nourish my heart and soul with prayer, the sacraments, and good books and media.

FRIDAY, SECOND WEEK OF LENT

Every day, I try to perform as many practices as I can, and I do all in my power not to let a single occasion pass by. I am saying at the bottom of my heart the little prayers which form the perfume of roses, as often as I can.

—Letters of Saint Thérèrese of Lisieux

Parent Reflection

Saint Thérèse loved to imagine planting flowers and roses as she performed sacrifices and said her prayers, imagining she was growing a garden filled with countless virtues to please Jesus. Often we think we have to accomplish great things to please God, but in reality he wants us to be faithful to our duties within our vocation. Impress upon the children the need to offer up sacrifices and prayers during this penitential season to please Jesus.

Family Prayer

All make the Sign of the Cross.

Parent: Dear Jesus, please accept our offering of prayer, fasting, and almsgiving today. Help us grow in holiness and love. Now let us listen to these words of Saint Thérèse.

A parent or child reads the opening quotation aloud.

All: Blessed Mother Mary, bring us closer to your Son, Jesus.

Saint Thérèse, please pray for us. Amen.

A Story from Saint Thérèse's Life

Thérèse's sister Pauline (Sister Agnes of Jesus) created a book of prayers with an embroidered cover (fashioned by one of the nuns) for Thérèse's preparation for First Communion. She enclosed a chaplet for Thérèse to count her acts of sacrifice. Pauline told Thérèse to "plant" many flowers so that Jesus will "find heaven in your child's heart." Thérèse committed herself to the task of "planting flowers" by offering many sacrifices and prayers with love to Jesus.

Fasting

Today, fast from rushing. If you are tempted to rush through prayers, good deeds, chores, or whatever, make a point to slow down (even a little) to savor the moment and offer it lovingly to God.

Almsgiving

Help the children draw ten simple flowers. Tell them they can color each one in as they say a prayer or perform an act of love or sacrifice today. The older children can use a chaplet or Rosary to count their prayers and sacrifices today. If time allows, make a string of beads or knots on a cord with the kids and help them count their loving acts.

Prayer

Today's Intention: Let us pray for peace in our world.

Closing Prayer: Dear Jesus, we love you. Please accept our little sacrifices.

All pray the Our Father, Hail Mary, and Glory Be.

All through the Day: God is happy when I turn to him.

THIRD SUNDAY OF LENT

> How can a soul as imperfect as mine aspire to the passion of
> the plentitude of Love? O Jesus, my first and only Friend,
> You whom I love uniquely, explain this mystery to me!
>
> —*Story of a Soul*

Parent Reflection

Today is the Third Sunday of Lent. All of the gospels for the Church's three-year cycle of readings, although different, invite us to a conversion of heart by remembering the words of Ash Wednesday: "Turn away from sin and be faithful to the Gospel."

Jesus offered the living water (Jn 4:5–42), inviting the Samaritan woman to repent of her sins and drink the living water to be truly converted. Jesus cleansed the Temple (Jn 2:13–25) and forcefully ejected the money changers. Jesus gives the example of the barren fig tree (Lk 13:1–9) to remind us of God's great patience with us even in our failures.

Saint Thérèse's words today speak about her imperfections yet emphasize the fact that despite them, God still calls her to the "plentitude of love." Saint Thérèse, although asking God for an explanation in her prayers, is heartily aware that everyone is called to conversion, to holiness. We are to offer everything in our lives to Jesus to release the hindrances (grudges, hurts, sin, misunderstandings) in our lives to free our hearts to receive God's love.

Family Prayer

All make the Sign of the Cross.

> *Parent*: Dear Jesus, we offer you our imperfections and our sins. We are sorry and want to amend our lives with the help of your love. Now let us listen to these words of Saint Thérèse.

A parent or child reads the opening quotation aloud.

All: Blessed Mother Mary, bring us closer to your Son, Jesus.

Saint Thérèse, please pray for us. Amen.

A Story from Saint Thérèse's Life

Three months after Thérèse was cured of her debilitating illness, her father took the family back to Alençon. Thérèse delighted in seeing all of the places she knew so well as a small child. She visited her mother's grave, asking her mother to protect her always. Thérèse believed that God gave her a special grace to know that the luxuries of the world, although enjoyable, were not to be sought after in place of serving God. She knew God wanted her to choose him freely, and she felt he gave her that distinctive time to be once again in her childhood town to ponder and pray before receiving her First Communion. Reflecting on the experience, she said, "The only good is to love God with all one's heart and to be poor in spirit here on earth" (*Story of a Soul*, 73).

Fasting

Today, fast from a luxury. For instance, choose one or more of these suggestions: take a shorter shower, eat a smaller portion in all your meals today, give up a dessert, serve others before yourself, commit to rise ten or fifteen minutes earlier tomorrow morning. Urge the kids to give up a treat or a fun pastime today.

Almsgiving

Give God thirty minutes of your time today for spiritual nourishment (reading, Catholic media, or quiet reflection and prayer). Pray a few extra prayers with the family at the dinner table and offer them for a needy person.

Prayer

> *Today's Intention*: Let's pray for all those who have left the Church.

Closing Prayer: Dear Jesus, please forgive us our sins and bring us close to you. Let our Christian lives be a shining light to all.

All pray the Our Father, Hail Mary, and Glory Be.

All through the Day: God wants to live in my heart.

Every day I made a large number of fervent acts which made up so many flowers, and I offered up an even greater number of aspirations. . . . These acts of love formed flower buds.

—*Story of a Soul*

Parent Reflection

Saint Thérèse was guided by her sister Pauline's prayer book to make use of every opportunity to show her love to Jesus in word and deed. Thérèse was particularly attracted to the child Jesus, whom she'd call "little Jesus," because she was young. Encourage the children to perform little acts of love for their family members to please Jesus. Ask them to speak to Jesus in simple aspirations during the day. Find opportunities to do this yourself. Also, schedule a time to bring the family to Confession sometime soon.

Family Prayer

All make the Sign of the Cross.

Parent: Dear Jesus, accept our simple love for you. Come into our hearts. Now let us listen to these words of Saint Thérèse.

A parent or child reads the opening quotation aloud.

All: Blessed Mother Mary, bring us closer to your Son, Jesus.

Saint Thérèse, please pray for us. Amen.

A Story from Saint Thérèse's Life

Thérèse told her sister Pauline that she had benefited much from the prayer book Pauline had made for her. When Thérèse saw in it a picture of the dove giving its heart to Jesus, she told Pauline, "Well! I, too, want to adorn my heart with all the beautiful flowers I will meet in order to offer it to little Jesus on the day of my First Communion, and I desire . . . that little Jesus be so pleased in my heart that he will not think of going back to heaven" (*Letters of Saint Thérèse of Lisieux*, volume 1, 190).

Fasting

Today, fast from saying or doing anything unkind.

Almsgiving

Encourage the children to say these (or their own) aspirations of Saint Thérèse throughout the day: "Little Jesus, I love you"; "Little Jesus, don't let me be proud anymore"; "My whole heart is yours, Jesus." Each time they pray them sincerely, with your assistance, they may put a flower (it can be paper, silk, or plastic) or a marble in a container on the kitchen table to count their prayers of love. Watch the container grow with "flowers."

Prayer

Today's Intention: Let us pray for all priests and religious.

Closing Prayer: Dear Jesus, mold my heart to love you more.

All pray the Our Father, Hail Mary, and Glory Be.

All through the Day: Jesus wants my heart. I will prepare it for him.

> Marie spoke to me about life's struggles and of the palm given to the victors . . . [and] eternal riches that one can so easily amass each day.
>
> —*Story of a Soul*

Parent Reflection

Our busy days can speed by and simply blend into the next with little or no thought about our duty to grow in holiness. We might be satisfied with merely going through the motions because we have too much to accomplish, yet it is essential to give thought to our spiritual lives and our responsibility to hand on the Faith to our children. Even simply planning time to ponder and pray throughout the day can create considerable, positive results in our hearts.

Family Prayer

All make the Sign of the Cross.

Parent: Dear Jesus, open our hearts to your love. Now let us listen to these words of Saint Thérèse.

A parent or child reads the opening quotation aloud.

All: Blessed Mother Mary, bring us closer to your Son, Jesus.

Saint Thérèse, please pray for us. Amen.

A Story from Saint Thérèse's Life

Thérèse's sister Marie taught her religion lessons because Pauline was at the convent. Marie impressed upon Thérèse that the way of becoming holy was through being faithful to the little things. Thérèse said, "I sat on her lap and listened eagerly to everything she said to me" (*Story of a Soul*, 74). Thérèse spent her spare time thinking and praying quietly and later realized that God was teaching her the art of mental prayer.

Fasting

Today, fast from wasting time. If you have free time, turn your thoughts to prayer as Saint Thérèse did.

Almsgiving

Give time away today by teaching the Faith in some way to a family member. Be an example of faith, tell a short story, or read a story of faith to the children.

Prayer

> *Today's Intention*: Let's pray for those without faith in God.
>
> *Closing Prayer*: Dear Lord, help our family be a witness of faith.
>
> *All pray the Our Father, Hail Mary, and Glory Be.*
>
> *All through the Day*: I should be mindful of how I spend my time.

And, truly, if I suffered very much at the boarding school, I was largely repaid by the ineffable happiness of those few days spent waiting for Jesus.

—*Story of a Soul*

Parent Reflection

Raising and caring for children means that, on any given day, anything can happen. Each day presents its joys and its challenges. Someone might suddenly become ill, the kids may get into trouble, or you might not feel up to snuff. You might be facing a job loss and financial difficulties. Any number of things can challenge us. Throughout the difficulties, we can always turn to prayer. God will grant us grace and courage. Ask God for that today.

Family Prayer

All make the Sign of the Cross.

Parent: Dear Jesus, please grant us much grace and courage to grow in holiness within our daily lives. Now let us listen to these words of Saint Thérèse.

A parent or child reads the opening quotation aloud.

All: Blessed Mother Mary, bring us closer to your Son, Jesus.

Saint Thérèse, please pray for us. Amen.

A Story from Saint Thérèse's Life

After three months of preparation and a special retreat, the long awaited day finally arrived: Thérèse made her First Holy Communion. She could hardly contain her emotion at the splendor in receiving Jesus for the first time, and tears flowed down her cheeks. Thérèse likened her experience to "a kiss of love." She said, "Ah! How sweet was that first kiss of Jesus!" Thérèse gave herself to Jesus at that moment and later that afternoon consecrated her life to the Blessed Virgin.

Fasting

Today, fast from idle chatter and gossip. Instead of wasting time chatting about nothing in particular, focus on spiritual nourishment. Let everything you say please God.

Almsgiving

Give time to Jesus today. Ask the kids and help them to write a poem to Jesus.

Prayer

Today's Intention: Pray for all those who are preparing to become Catholic at Easter.

Closing Prayer: Dear Lord Jesus, help us learn to appreciate you more.

All pray the Our Father, Hail Mary, and Glory Be.

All through the Day: Jesus loves me.

Jesus, Jesus, if I wanted to write all my desires, I would have to borrow your Book of Life, for in it are reported all the actions of all the saints, and I would accomplish all of them for you.

—Story of a Soul

Parent Reflection

Your family is making its way along the Lenten journey. Take a moment today to think about your progress. Are you all preparing your hearts for Jesus as Saint Thérèse did? Can you strive to emulate her zeal for pleasing Jesus? Talk to the children about pleasing Jesus with their words and actions. Ask them to try to do everything with love.

Family Prayer

All make the Sign of the Cross.

> *Parent*: Dear Jesus, increase the desire of our hearts to serve you. Now let us listen to these words of Saint Thérèse.

A parent or child reads the opening quotation aloud.

> *All*: Blessed Mother Mary, bring us closer to your Son, Jesus.

Saint Thérèse, please pray for us. Amen.

A Story from Saint Thérèse's Life

Shortly after Thérèse's First Communion, she prepared to receive the Holy Spirit in Confirmation. She returned to taking lessons at the Abbey boarding school, which she was not particularly fond of. Thérèse didn't share much in common with the children who were disobedient or rude, but she practiced the virtues when dealing with these challenges.

Fasting

Today, fast from complaining. Try to see each challenge today as a blessing. It may be hard, but ask God for the grace to accomplish it.

Almsgiving

Encourage the children to count their blessings—to actually jot down (or draw) the good things in their lives with pencil and paper (or crayons).

Prayer

Today's Intention: Let's pray for all who are struggling in some way.

Closing Prayer: Dear Jesus, keep us close to your Sacred Heart.

All pray the Our Father, Hail Mary, and Glory Be.

All through the Day: Jesus wants us to love with his love.

FRIDAY, THIRD WEEK OF LENT

> If during my life I could have suffered to offer one soul to God, one soul that would be snatched from the fire of hell. Oh! How happy I would be. Really, how could one complain about sufferings when one sees the fruit of suffering.
> —*Letters of Saint Thérèse of Lisieux*

Parent Reflection

The season of Lent, as we know, is meant to be penitential. Perhaps we shouldn't be surprised when things don't go as smoothly as planned, even doing these simple exercises with your family. Use this season to try to master your impatience, anger, irritability, and any vice that gets in the way of leading a virtuous life. When you are tempted to react to something harshly, turn your attention immediately to praying for the virtues you need. You can teach the children to be virtuous in the same way. Remember, we are all a work in progress—we do not have sparkling halos yet! It takes time. God will grant us the graces we need, and as Saint Thérèse points out, lovingly offering suffering to God can help save souls.

Family Prayer

All make the Sign of the Cross.

> *Parent*: Dear Jesus, I'm sorry for complaining about my sufferings. Now let us listen to these words of Saint Thérèse.

A parent or child reads the opening quotation aloud.

> *All*: Blessed Mother Mary, bring us closer to your Son, Jesus.

> Saint Thérèse, please pray for us. Amen.

A Story from Saint Thérèse's Life

Soon after Thérèse made her First Communion, she began to realize that Jesus was allowing her to suffer inconveniences or misunderstandings in her life. She could offer them to him with love to merit graces and help save souls. Things that would ordinarily have satisfied her heart no longer were as meaningful to her. She began to discover solace only in her prayers to Jesus, Mary, and the saints. She spent time praying to Jesus in the Blessed Sacrament whenever she could.

Fasting

Today, fast from feeling sorry for yourself.

Almsgiving

Offer comfort to others today. Be on the lookout for those who need encouragement. Make a phone call with the kids to a lonely relative or neighbor to cheer him or her.

Prayer

Today's Intention: Let's pray for all those who live alone and those who are suffering.

Closing Prayer: Dear Jesus, thank you for my life, just as it is.

All pray the Our Father, Hail Mary, and Glory Be.

All through the Day: I shouldn't waste my suffering.

FOURTH SUNDAY OF LENT

On that *luminous* night which sheds such light on the delights of the Holy Trinity, Jesus, the gentle, a little Child of only one hour, changed the night of my soul into rays of light.

—*Story of a Soul*

Parent Reflection

Today is the fourth Sunday of Lent. The gospel readings from all three cycles of Lent offer perspectives on Jesus, the Light of the World. The story of the man born blind (Jn 9:1–41; Cycle A) speaks to us about faith. The faithful man receives physical and spiritual sight while those around him remain "blind" and lacking in faith. Nicodemus (Jn 3:14–21; Cycle B) sought out Jesus in the night because he was afraid. Nonetheless, Jesus explained to Nicodemus, "Whoever lives in truth comes to the light, so that his works may be clearly seen as done in God." The parable of the prodigal son (Lk 15:1–3, 11–32; Cycle C) illustrates a wayward son who sees the "light" and returns his father's mercy. His brother is "blind" to his own selfishness and his father's mercy. In her words for today, Saint Thérèse speaks of how the light of Jesus, even Jesus as a gentle little child, brought peace and comfort to her soul.

Family Prayer

All make the Sign of the Cross.

> *Parent:* Dear Jesus, we seek the light of your love. Now let us listen to these words of Saint Thérèse.

A parent or child reads the opening quotation aloud.

> *All:* Blessed Mother Mary, bring us closer to your Son, Jesus.

> Saint Thérèse, please pray for us. Amen.

A Story from Saint Thérèse's Life

The youngest child in her family, Thérèse was accustomed to being cared for and pampered. She was very sensitive and cried easily. She knew she had to mature before she could enter the convent. In fact, she concluded that God would need to work a miracle in her heart. When Thérèse was about ten years old, she received her miracle. She and her family came home from midnight Mass on Christmas in 1886 and Thérèse went to fetch her shoes. Thérèse overheard her fatigued father express to her sister Celine with annoyance that this thankfully would be the last year of placing little presents in Thérèse's shoes (as was the custom of their childhood). Normally, Thérèse would have cried. Instead, she forced back her tears and joyfully withdrew the trinkets from her shoes, convinced that through God's grace she had instantly matured.

Fasting

Today, fast from being prideful. If you are tempted to boast, say a prayer: "Jesus, help me." In everything today, try to give praise or credit to someone else.

Almsgiving

Think about someone in your family, neighborhood, or school who needs encouragement. Endeavor to compliment him or her for his or her accomplishments. Say a prayer for that person today.

Prayer

Today's Intention: Let's pray for all families around the world.

Closing Prayer: Dear Jesus, thank you for lighting up my life. Help me to offer your light to others.

All pray the Our Father, Hail Mary, and Glory Be.

All through the Day: I will strive to light up others' lives.

On that *night of light* began the third period of my life, the most beautiful and the most filled with graces from heaven. The work I had been unable to do in ten years was done by Jesus in one instant.

—Story of a Soul

Parent Reflection

At times, we parents may feel discouraged by today's darkened culture and the challenges it brings. No matter how depressing or dismal the world outside our domestic church's doors may seem, though, God continues to give us hope as well as the courage to continue striving to be a luminous torch to light the way for our children. Throughout the day, ponder ways in which you can be a light of faith to your family.

Family Prayer

All make the Sign of the Cross.

Parent: Dear Jesus, help us to be strong and prayerful amid the forces of the world that contradict our Christianity. Now let us listen to these words of Saint Thérèse.

A parent or child reads the opening quotation aloud.

All: Blessed Mother Mary, bring us closer to your Son, Jesus.

Saint Thérèse, please pray for us. Amen.

A Story from Saint Thérèse's Life

Thérèse sensed charity entering her soul as she matured in her faith. She wanted to forget about her own pleasures and desired to serve others, which made her truly happy. She experienced a longing to help convert sinners' souls. One day, as Thérèse was praying and looking at a picture of Jesus hanging from the Cross, she experienced a twinge of sorrow, envisioning Jesus' Precious Blood dripping down from one of his sacred hands and falling on the ground. She prayed that she could "catch" his Blood by remaining in spirit at the foot of the Cross.

Fasting

Fast from a treat today.

Almsgiving

Encourage the children to surprise someone today with an unexpected gift of charity. Give them some ideas.

Prayer

Today's Intention: Let's pray for families who are grieving for one of their family members.

Closing Prayer: Dear Jesus, enlarge our hearts to receive your great love.

All pray the Our Father, Hail Mary, and Glory Be.

All through the Day: Jesus gave his life for me.

TUESDAY, FOURTH WEEK OF LENT

O God hidden in the prison of the tabernacle! I come with joy to you each evening to thank you for the graces you have given me. I ask pardon for the faults I committed today, which has just slipped away like a dream. . . .

—*The Prayers of Saint Thérèse of Lisieux*

Parent Reflection

Saint Thérèse got on her knees each night to thank God for his blessings and ask forgiveness for her shortcomings. She also prayed throughout the day, but she made a point of meeting with Jesus before she closed her eyes. Our lives in the family are very busy, but if we don't pause to acknowledge the Lord in our life, what good is all of what we are trying to do? Take some time this week to impress upon the children the need to make room for Jesus in their lives. Guide them to a deeper prayer life. Bring them to the Blessed Sacrament whenever you are able.

Family Prayer

All make the Sign of the Cross.

> *Parent:* Dear Jesus, we love you. Help us to slow down and spend time with you. Now let us listen to these words of Saint Thérèse.

A parent or child reads the opening quotation aloud.

> *All:* Blessed Mother Mary, bring us closer to your Son, Jesus.

Saint Thérèse, please pray for us. Amen.

A Story from Saint Thérèse's Life

Thérèse's desire to save souls grew intensely each day. She seemed to hear the words that Jesus spoke to the Samaritan woman: "Give me a drink!" She wanted to quench his thirst. Thérèse interpreted his words to mean she should pray for sinners. Her heart was comforted each time she offered sinners to Jesus, asking him to purify the stains of sins with his Precious Blood.

Fasting

Fast from excuses today. When you might be tempted to make an excuse, pause and ponder how you might accomplish the task without complaint.

Almsgiving

Today, try to give more attention to your work, your chores, and your encounters with everyone. Thank God for everything!

Prayer

Today's Intention: Let's pray for all those we might have hurt in some way.

Closing Prayer: Dear Lord, grant me the graces I need to come closer to you.

All pray the Our Father, Hail Mary, and Glory Be.

All through the Day: God wants me to keep company with him.

WEDNESDAY, FOURTH WEEK OF LENT

The cry of Jesus on the Cross sounded continually in my heart: "I thirst!" These words ignited within me an unknown and very living fire.

—Story of a Soul

Parent Reflection

Parenting is no easy task. It could be easier if we forgot about our values and did not worry about our fundamental responsibilities to raise little saints. Sadly, many parents today just go with the flow of society and are not vigilant in shielding their kids from the dark pastimes of the culture and pointing them toward God. We must take our unique role seriously. We need to pray for the strength and grace to do our jobs to the best of our ability. God is counting on us.

Family Prayer

All make the Sign of the Cross.

Parent: Dear Jesus, grant us the grace to desire to quench your thirst with our acts of love in our family. Now let us listen to these words of Saint Thérèse.

A parent or child reads the opening quotation aloud.

All: Blessed Mother Mary, bring us closer to your Son, Jesus.

Saint Thérèse, please pray for us. Amen.

A Story from Saint Thérèse's Life

Thérèse grew closer to her sister Celine. Since that momentous Christmas when Thérèse matured mystically, Celine considered Thérèse grown-up enough to understand deep truths of the faith. Before that, to Thérèse's dismay, Celine told Thérèse she was "too little." They became spiritual sisters, and their thoughts were constantly lifted to heaven.

Fasting

Fast from squabbles. Tell the children to be on perfect behavior today—no arguing and better listening.

Almsgiving

Encourage the children to do something charitable for someone in the family today: help with homework, do an extra chore, or perform a random act of kindness.

Prayer

Today's Intention: Let's pray for orphans and the unwanted.

Closing Prayer: Dear Lord, please increase our desire to learn more about you.

All pray the Our Father, Hail Mary, and Glory Be.

All through the Day: Jesus, I trust in you!

I wanted to give my Beloved to drink and I felt myself consumed with a thirst for souls . . . those of great sinners. I burned with the desire to snatch them from the eternal flames.

—Story of a Soul

Parent Reflection

Life in a family is not always a picnic. Many times it can be challenging to get through a day without feeling like we could blow a gasket! Our good Lord offers us so many opportunities to surrender our hearts to him rather than surrender to our feelings. We can merit many graces and please God by ignoring insults from others, by choosing the high road when we'd rather make a comment, by praying instead of losing our cool, and other patient acts. Is it any wonder why families are a mixture of personalities? God wants us to grow together in holiness through forgiveness and love.

Family Prayer

All make the Sign of the Cross.

> *Parent*: Dear Jesus, fill our hearts with your love. Now let us listen to these words of Saint Thérèse.

A parent or child reads the opening quotation aloud.

> *All*: Blessed Mother Mary, bring us closer to your Son, Jesus.

Saint Thérèse, please pray for us. Amen.

A Story from Saint Thérèse's Life

As Thérèse busied herself with praying for the souls of sinners, she heard the news of a great criminal condemned to death for unspeakable crimes. It seemed he would die without confessing his ill deeds. Thérèse was determined to do all in her power to pray for him, offering all of the infinite merits of Jesus to God. She also begged her sister

Celine to have a Mass said for him. The instant before the man's execution, he suddenly grabbed the crucifix held out to him by the priest and kissed it three times. Thérèse was convinced that her prayers were instrumental in the man's decision to profess that dramatic statement of repentance and surrender before his death.

Fasting

Fast from defending yourself today.

Almsgiving

Give away compliments and smiles to everyone you encounter today—everyone!

Prayer

> *Today's Intention*: Let's pray for all those who are in danger of dying without confessing their sins.
>
> *Closing Prayer*: Dear Jesus, help me to make a difference in others' lives.
>
> *All pray the Our Father, Hail Mary, and Glory Be.*
>
> *All through the Day*: God grants us many graces. We are to use them for his glory.

Oh! How I love the memory of the blessed days of my child-hood . . . to protect the flower of my innocence the Lord always surrounded me with love!

—*The Poetry of Saint Thérèse of Lisieux*

Parent Reflection

Saint Thérèse was convinced that because she was surrounded with love and the concern of her family, she remained virtuous. We can all learn from the holy Martin family and work at instilling holiness in the hearts of our own children. Saint Thérèse's parents, Zélie and Louis, have been declared "blessed" by the Church and their daughter declared a saint and Doctor of the Church. The Martins sure did something right in raising their children!

Family Prayer

All make the Sign of the Cross.

Parent: Dear Jesus, please unite our hearts in prayer, now and always. Now let us listen to these words of Saint Thérèse.

A parent or child reads the opening quotation aloud.

All: Blessed Mother Mary, bring us closer to your Son, Jesus.

Saint Thérèse, please pray for us. Amen.

A Story from Saint Thérèse's Life

As Jesus granted Thérèse many graces and she grew in holiness, Thérèse thought about a way she could break the news to her father about her deep desire and calling from God to become a Carmelite nun. She was only fourteen, and her papa had already allowed three of his daughters to ascend the hill to Carmel. Thérèse wanted to spare him any pain but also knew that she had to tell him.

Fasting

Fast from worry today. Give all of your worries and concerns to God in prayer.

Almsgiving

Today, give away a kind word or deed and put a lot of love into your actions.

Prayer

Today's Intention: Let's pray for those called to religious life to be open to God's graces. Let's pray for their families as well.

Closing Prayer: Dear Lord Jesus, enkindle in my heart the fire of your love and help me spread it to others.

All pray the Our Father, Hail Mary, and Glory Be.

All through the Day: God has a mission for me.

FIFTH SUNDAY OF LENT

> For a long time I have drunk from the chalice of tears. I have shared your cup of sorrows, and I have understood that suffering has its charms, that by the Cross we save sinners.
>
> *—The Poetry of Saint Thérèse of Lisieux*

Parent Reflection

Today is the fifth Sunday in Lent. In the gospels for the three cycles, we marvel at the raising of Lazarus (Jn 11:1–45; Cycle A), we hear Jesus speak of his coming death (Jn 12:20–33; Cycle B), and we listen to the story of the woman caught in adultery (Jn 8:1–11; Cycle C).

Jesus teaches us that we all must rise from our sin to new life. He says in John 12, "Amen, amen, I say to you, unless a grain of wheat falls to the ground and dies, it remains just a grain of wheat; but if it dies, it produces fruit." The raising of Lazarus was a sign of this new life. He was not resurrected as Jesus was, but nonetheless, he was resuscitated. It points to Jesus' rising and the power of Christ to raise us up out of our sin to new life. The woman caught in adultery was also raised to a new life. Jesus' love and immense mercy saved her physically and, more importantly, his forgiveness gave her new life.

Saint Thérèse teaches us to remain faithful to God throughout our struggles. Jesus tells us, "unless a grain of wheat falls to the ground and dies," it will not bear fruit. What is the lesson here? We always have the ability to turn to God. We meditate on Jesus' sufferings and death on the Cross. We are reminded that even Jesus, who was God, struggled and suffered, but look what came of his great suffering! We too are called to live heroic lives. Through the challenges in life, we can pray to be a Christian example, inspiring others to come closer to God. We can gain strength through the sacraments, especially Confession and the Eucharist.

Family Prayer

All make the Sign of the Cross.

Parent: Dear Jesus, forgive us of our sins and draw us close to you. Now let us listen to these words of Saint Thérèse.

A parent or child reads the opening quotation aloud.

> *All*: Blessed Mother Mary, bring us closer to your Son, Jesus.
>
> Saint Thérèse, please pray for us. Amen.

A Story from Saint Thérèse's Life

Desiring to enter Carmel, Thérèse seemed plagued with many trials she was required to pass through. Thérèse was so determined to follow God's call that she said if forced to pass through flames, she would do it out of love for Jesus. Even telling her dear papa her blessed plans was painful. On the Feast of Pentecost, Thérèse begged prayers from the saints to help her choose just the right words. Finally, out in the garden, Thérèse sat beside her father and, with misty eyes, poured out her deepest desire to him. Louis became quiet and reflective. He then plucked a little white flower from the ground and handed it to Thérèse, explaining how God preserves the flowers.

Fasting

Brainstorm together your fasting plans for the week. Decide what you can do together as a family (and individually too).

Almsgiving

Together, make a list of three ideas on how your family can offer help to someone in need this week. Choose one to carry out this week.

Prayer

> *Today's Intention*: Let's pray for those who are sad or lonely.
>
> *Closing Prayer*: Dear Lord Jesus, let our prayers bring forth fruits.
>
> *All pray the Our Father, Hail Mary, and Glory Be.*
>
> *All through the Day*: I need to rise from my sins.

I accept with gratitude the thorns mingled with the flowers.
—*The Poetry of Saint Thérèse of Lisieux*

Parent Reflection

The penitential season of Lent is supposed to be, well, penitential. Saint Thérèse's statement of happily accepting the thorns along with the flowers may seem appropriate for her, but that same attitude is one we should also embrace. We know that life is not only about pretty roses. Thorns are a necessary part of the picture as well. Saint Thérèse was deeply prayerful, and because she was, she could accept all of the sufferings in her life as somehow part of God's holy will for her amid the deepest of joys she also experienced. With Holy Week fast approaching, take some time to ponder the struggles in your life. How can you unite your sufferings to Jesus' Passion and Death on the Cross?

Family Prayer

All make the Sign of the Cross.

> *Parent*: Dear Jesus, help me to surrender my whole life to you. Now let us listen to these words of Saint Thérèse.

A parent or child reads the opening quotation aloud.

> *All*: Blessed Mother Mary, bring us closer to your Son, Jesus.

> Saint Thérèse, please pray for us. Amen.

A Story from Saint Thérèse's Life

With her father's approval to join her sisters in the convent, Thérèse's heart soared. She was thrilled that she would enter Carmel in God's perfect timing. Next, Thérèse sought the approval of her uncle who had helped to raise her, but he forbade her to talk about her vocation any more to him until she was seventeen. He thought going into

Carmel at fifteen years old was much too soon. This sent Thérèse into a painful trial. She overcame her sorrow with prayer. After a few days, Thérèse's uncle had a miraculous change of heart and told Thérèse she was a "little flower God wanted to gather."

Fasting

Today, fast from a little comfort—an extra portion of food, extra sleep tomorrow morning, time to yourself, and so on.

Almsgiving

Give away your personal time. Sacrifice some of your free time to give to someone else today.

Prayer

Today's Intention: Let's pray for families everywhere.

Closing Prayer: Dear Jesus, open our hearts to those in need.

All pray the Our Father, Hail Mary, and Glory Be.

All through the Day: With God's grace, I can make a positive difference in someone's life.

When God stretches out His hand to ask, His hand is never empty.

—Story of a Soul

Parent Reflection

Saint Thérèse was sure that when God asks something of us, he will provide the courage and strength we need to fulfill his calling. Today, try to look at everything in that light. Help the children to recognize that God is always with us, even when things are tough. God will give us all the grace we need to follow his holy will in our lives.

Family Prayer

All make the Sign of the Cross.

Parent: Dear Jesus, thank you for your abiding presence in our lives. Now let us listen to these words of Saint Thérèse.

A parent or child reads the opening quotation aloud.

All: Blessed Mother Mary, bring us closer to your Son, Jesus.

Saint Thérèse, please pray for us. Amen.

A Story from Saint Thérèse's Life

With the consent of her papa, uncle, and aunt to enter religious life, Thérèse felt extremely close to her blessed goal. Her heart was lighter, and joy exuded from her face. Next, Thérèse was off to Carmel to meet with her sister Pauline, who shared the sad news with her younger sister that the priest superior would not give his consent for Thérèse's entrance into Carmel until she was twenty-one years old. It just couldn't be true! Refusing to lose hope, Thérèse headed to the rectory with Papa and Celine, but nothing would change the bishop's mind. Thérèse left the rectory in a torrent of rain, her umbrella hiding her tears.

Fasting

Today, fast from losing hope. Anytime you feel discouraged, turn to hope and prayer. Help the children to understand the importance of this deliberate effort.

Almsgiving

Give love away. Ponder ways to show your love to the family and neighbors, especially the downcast or those facing difficulties.

Prayer

Today's Intention: Let's pray for vocations to religious life.

Closing Prayer: Dear Lord, fill my heart with hope and help me give it to others.

All pray the Our Father, Hail Mary, and Glory Be.

All through the Day: Jesus will provide all I need. I should trust him.

My little boat is having trouble reaching port! For a long time, I have seen the shore and always I find myself far off, but it is Jesus who is guiding. . . . When he wills it, it will be able to approach the port safely. . . . God is sending me these trials.

—Letters of Saint Thérèse of Lisieux

Parent Reflection

How many times, even in the course of one day, might we feel tempted to give up on something? If it's something worthwhile and God wills it, we should never give up. We need to be prayerful, patient, and persevering. We can imitate Saint Thérèse, committing to follow God's will by being trustful and patient when it seems like the "boat" is having trouble getting to "shore."

Family Prayer

All make the Sign of the Cross.

Parent: Dear Jesus, grant us courage, patience, and strength to do your holy will. Now let us listen to these words of Saint Thérèse.

A parent or child reads the opening quotation aloud.

All: Blessed Mother Mary, bring us closer to your Son, Jesus.

Saint Thérèse, please pray for us. Amen.

A Story from Saint Thérèse's Life

Thérèse was determined to beg the bishop and the Holy Father too, if need be, to enter Carmel at fifteen years old. She would not give up! Being a prayerful soul, she continued to walk in faith despite the obstacles. Torrents of rain were falling again when Thérèse and Papa arrived at Bayeau to see the bishop and to plead her cause. Thérèse earnestly prayed for the grace to express clearly her reasons for seeking entrance into Carmel. The moment arrived, and Thérèse spoke to the bishop. His response was not what she hoped for. He told Thérèse that he couldn't approve her request before he interviewed the superior of Carmel. Again, Thérèse shed tears but felt God's peace too because she was seeking his will, not hers.

Fasting

Today, fast from a special treat. Help the children decide what to give up.

Almsgiving

Give away your smiles today. Ask the kids to make a smiley picture to give to someone they know.

Prayer

> *Today's Intention*: Let's pray for the Church and all its members, especially the souls in purgatory.
>
> *Closing Prayer*: Dear Jesus, grant me the graces that I need.
>
> *All pray the Our Father, Hail Mary, and Glory Be.*
>
> *All through the Day*: God will give me peace, even during the storms in life.

THURSDAY, FIFTH WEEK OF LENT

Without love, deeds, even the most brilliant, count as nothing.

—*Story of a Soul*

Parent Reflection

Have you ever heard the statement, "If Mama ain't happy, ain't nobody happy"? Of course, this is not proper grammar, but the point remains that mothers and fathers need to radiate joy and love in the hearts of their homes. Children pick up on our moods and behaviors. Even when life is demanding, try to find reasons to be joyful and teach your children to do the same.

Family Prayer

All make the Sign of the Cross.

Parent: Dear Jesus, bring love and joy to our hearts. Now let us listen to these words of Saint Thérèse.

A parent or child reads the opening quotation aloud.

All: Blessed Mother Mary, bring us closer to your Son, Jesus.

Saint Thérèse, please pray for us. Amen.

A Story from Saint Thérèse's Life

Off to Rome, the Eternal City! Thérèse traveled with Papa and Celine in the jubilee year of Pope Leo XIII and prayed to the Blessed Mother and Saint Joseph to watch over her. After the Pontiff's Mass and the Mass of thanksgiving, Thérèse and the others would have a brief moment to kneel before the pope during his audience. Even though it was forbidden to speak to him, Thérèse was determined to beg his assistance to enter Carmel at the age of fifteen. When the time came, she cried out to the Holy Father. Pope Leo told Thérèse to do as the superiors tell her, and if it is God's will, she would enter Carmel. Thérèse hesitated and remained kneeling at the Pontiff's feet, which caused the guards to forcibly lift her to her feet and escort her out.

Tears again filled her eyes, yet Thérèse felt peace in the bottom of her heart.

Fasting

Fast from some technology today. It's hard, but try to avoid unnecessary time watching television, playing video games, and surfing the Internet.

Almsgiving

Give Jesus an extra ten minutes of time today. Ask him in prayer how you can help others. Endeavor to reach out in charity.

Prayer

Today's Intention: Let's pray for children all around the word.

Closing Prayer: Dear Lord, prepare our hearts to receive you more deeply this upcoming Holy Week.

All pray the Our Father, Hail Mary, and Glory Be.

All through the Day: Jesus wants my heart.

FRIDAY, FIFTH WEEK OF LENT

I find that trials help very much in detaching us from this earth. They make us look higher than this world. Here below, nothing can satisfy us. We cannot enjoy a little rest except in being ready to do God's will.

—*Letters of Saint Thérèse of Lisieux*

Parent Reflection

Since it's a Lenten Friday, endeavor to foster a more penitential atmosphere in your home today. Make an effort to achieve silence as much as you can. Of course, the household will be filled with sounds of life, but try to do without an excess of chatter, television, and video games. Get the children involved in wholesome activities.

Family Prayer

All make the Sign of the Cross.

Parent: Dear Jesus, prepare our hearts to come closer to you. Now let us listen to these words of Saint Thérèse.

A parent or child reads the opening quotation aloud.

All: Blessed Mother Mary, bring us closer to your Son, Jesus.

Saint Thérèse, please pray for us. Amen.

A Story from Saint Thérèse's Life

Pope Leo XIII did not give Thérèse the answer she sought. Thérèse now felt that all her hope should be placed in God alone; she had to pray and wait. Visiting with her sister Pauline at the convent in Carmel after returning from Rome comforted Thérèse, who poured her heart out to Pauline. Christmas arrived and Thérèse felt crushed that she was not at Carmel as she had planned, but amid the sorrow, she was convinced that God was allowing her to grow in her faith as she offered her suffering to him. She continued to wait.

Fasting

Fast from all treats today.

Almsgiving

Today, ask each of the children to do an extra age-appropriate chore and to pray as they do it.

Prayer

Today's Intention: Let's pray for all those in war-torn areas.

Closing Prayer: Dear Lord, accept our humble prayers. Fill us with your love.

All pray the Our Father, Hail Mary, and Glory Be.

All through the Day: My hope should be placed in God alone.

PASSION (PALM) SUNDAY

Joy isn't found in the material objects surrounding us but in the inner recesses of the soul.

—*Story of a Soul*

Parent Reflection

Palm Sunday, or Passion Sunday, is the last Sunday in our Lenten journey. We commemorate this important day, recalling its significance in salvation history: Jesus' triumphant entry into Jerusalem to celebrate the Passover. As Jesus rode in on a donkey, the people of Jerusalem rushed to greet him, recognizing him as their king. They laid a path of palm branches before him, saying, "Hosanna to the Son of David: Blessed is he who comes in the name of the Lord! Hosanna in the highest heaven!" (Mt 21:9).

Zechariah's prophecy was fulfilled as Jesus rode on a donkey: "See your king shall come to you; a just savior is he, meek. And riding on an ass, on a colt, the foal of an ass" (Zec 9:9). The donkey symbolized peace; the palm branches signified that a dignitary or king was triumphantly arriving. Palm branches have represented joy and victory down through the ages. They have been used in procession on Palm Sunday and distributed among the faithful to be displayed in their homes in special places and used as sacramentals. Palms were sometimes thrown into fires during storms and have been placed on graves, in barns, and in fields. Ashes from the burned, blessed palms are used for the following year on Ash Wednesday.

Holy Week begins with our reading of the Passion at Mass today. The coming week is a fitting time to pause to meditate on the events of the Passion. Many graces await us during this holiest of weeks. Participate in as many services at church this week as you can, receiving Jesus in the Eucharist.

Family Prayer

All make the Sign of the Cross.

Parent: Dear Jesus, we love you. We want to come closer to you. Now let us listen to these words of Saint Thérèse.

A parent or child reads the opening quotation aloud.

All: Blessed Mother Mary, bring us closer to your Son, Jesus.

Saint Thérèse, please pray for us. Amen.

A Story from Saint Thérèse's Life

On New Year's Day in 1888, Thérèse got word from Mother Marie Gonzague that the bishop finally had given his response regarding her entrance into Carmel: it would be delayed until after Lent. Thérèse burst into tears; she simply couldn't bear to wait another three months. Thérèse decided to practice little mortifications, little sacrifices in preparation to enter Carmel. The time passed, rich with many graces for Thérèse.

Fasting

Fast from whining today. If something disappoints you, offer it to God and trust him with it.

Almsgiving

Give away your concerns to God. Trust him more fully with your life starting right now!

Prayer

Today's Intention: Let's pray for all those who have no one to pray for them.

Closing Prayer: Dear Lord, please help us to care lovingly for those you place near us.

All pray the Our Father, Hail Mary, and Glory Be.

All through the Day: God's graces are awaiting me.

MONDAY OF HOLY WEEK

I desire only one thing when I shall be in Carmel, and it is to suffer always for Jesus. Life passes so quickly that really it must be better to have a very beautiful crown and a little trouble than to have an ordinary one without any trouble. . . . In suffering we can save souls.

—*Letters of Saint Thérèse of Lisieux*

Parent Reflection

Thérèse was certain of the value in offering her sufferings to God. She knew in her heart that, in her simple, loving way and with God's grace, she could actually help to save souls. So often we waste our suffering by grumbling and complaining. Saint Thérèse's example encourages us to be more generous and prayerful. As you dive in to this Holy Week, consider how you might earn the "beautiful crown" Thérèse mentions by offering your troubles and sacrifices to God. Teach the children to be thankful for their lives, challenges and all.

Family Prayer

All make the Sign of the Cross.

> *Parent:* Dear Jesus, help us to recognize the importance of making sacrifices for others and offering our lives to you. Now let us listen to these words of Saint Thérèse.

A parent or child reads the opening quotation aloud.

> *All:* Blessed Mother Mary, bring us closer to your Son, Jesus.

Saint Thérèse, please pray for us. Amen.

A Story from Saint Thérèse's Life

After appealing to the mother superior, the priest chaplain, the bishop, and finally the pope, the persistent Thérèse would get her way. In 1888, at the tender age of fifteen, she entered the convent, joining her older sisters in the cloistered Carmelite community.

Fasting

Today, fast from complaining about inconveniences and little sufferings. Say a prayer instead.

Almsgiving

Give some time today to pray for the souls in purgatory as well as all those who have turned their backs on God.

Prayer

Today's Intention: Let's pray for all of the souls in purgatory, especially priests and religious who don't have anyone to pray for them.

Closing Prayer: Dear Lord Jesus, thank you for our lives and the great gift of faith.

All pray the Our Father, Hail Mary, and Glory Be.

All through the Day: My prayers and sacrifices are important and can help save souls.

TUESDAY OF HOLY WEEK

Lord, what does it matter if the future is gloomy? To pray for tomorrow, oh no, I cannot! Keep my heart pure, cover me with your shadow just for today.

—The Poetry of Saint Thérèse of Lisieux

Parent Reflection

It's easy to worry about tomorrow rather than plant our feet firmly in today. Saint Thérèse's words above remind us to live in the moment. Today, try your best to really live in the moment. Communicate as much as you can with the family about the holiness of this week. During your prayer times together, strive to bring your hearts closer to Jesus.

Family Prayer

All make the Sign of the Cross.

Parent: Dear Jesus, please keep our hearts pure and help us turn to you in all of our needs. Now let us listen to these words of Saint Thérèse.

A parent or child reads the opening quotation aloud.

All: Blessed Mother Mary, bring us closer to your Son, Jesus.

Saint Thérèse, please pray for us. Amen.

A Story from Saint Thérèse's Life

The momentous day arrived for Thérèse to leave her childhood behind and enter the convent. It was April 9, 1888. She spent the night before with her family, sitting around the family table at *Les Buissonnets.* Everyone showered tenderness on her amid tears. The family attended Mass on the morning of Thérèse's entrance. Afterward, Thérèse's father bestowed his blessing on bended knees, tears flowing down his cheeks as he handed over his youngest daughter to God. The relatives sobbed, but Thérèse didn't shed a tear; her heart was full of joy. She embraced her relatives, passed through the convent doors, and was welcomed by the nuns. Thérèse's heart beat wildly. Suddenly, a deep and abiding peace filled her heart, a peace that would always remain with her.

Fasting

Fast from procrastination. If you need to do something, do it.

Almsgiving

Encourage the children to draw a picture or write a short, uplifting verse or story that they will give to someone on Easter Sunday.

Prayer

Today's Intention: Let us pray for all missionaries.

Closing Prayer: Dear Lord, keep us always close to your Sacred Heart.

All pray the Our Father, Hail Mary, and Glory Be.

All through the Day: Jesus wants me to pray for our needs today and not worry about tomorrow.

WEDNESDAY OF HOLY WEEK

Silence does good to the soul.

—Letters of Saint Thérèse of Lisieux

Parent Reflection

It's good to find some silence during Holy Week. Endeavor to make it your best Holy Week ever by taking the time to pray and meditate on Jesus' Passion, Death, and finally his Resurrection on Sunday morning. Foster a holy atmosphere in your domestic church. Continue to emphasize to the children the need to spend quiet time in prayer when possible.

Family Prayer

All make the Sign of the Cross.

> *Parent*: Dear Jesus, bless our family with your love and graces. Help us to become saints. Now let us listen to these words of Saint Thérèse.

A parent or child reads the opening quotation aloud.

> *All*: Blessed Mother Mary, bring us closer to your Son, Jesus.
>
> Saint Thérèse, please pray for us. Amen.

A Story from Saint Thérèse's Life

Thérèse immediately embraced her new life in the convent; her dream was fulfilled. She practiced little penances—doing the jobs forgotten by other sisters, not making excuses for things, depriving herself of comforts and conveniences. In January, Thérèse received her habit in a ceremony at Carmel. She was thrilled that her father had recovered from his stroke and could partake in her joy. He was admired by everyone for willingly giving all of his daughters to God. To Thérèse's delight, a light snow fell on the monastery garden, bringing a distinctive beauty to the momentous day.

Fasting

Fast from activity today when possible. Look for quiet times to pray.

Almsgiving

Give your heart to Jesus all day long. Whisper prayers to him. Tell him you love him.

Prayer

Today's Intention: Let's pray for the souls in purgatory, especially the forgotten ones.

Closing Prayer: Dear Jesus, we love you!

All pray the Our Father, Hail Mary, and Glory Be.

All through the Day: My life should become a prayer of love.

HOLY THURSDAY

> I would so much like to love Him! Love Him more than He has ever been loved! My only desire is to do the will of Jesus always! To dry away the little tears that sinners make Him shed.
>
> —*Letters of Saint Thérèse of Lisieux*

Parent Reflection

Today, we remember the Last Supper and the institution of both the Eucharist and the priesthood. Take time to ponder the great significance of Holy Thursday in your life as a Catholic. Talk to the children about these great events of our Faith that occurred on that momentous day a couple thousand years ago. Saint Thérèse's words above inspire us to love Jesus with all of our heart and follow his will. We too can imitate Saint Thérèse's "little way" by being faithful to our own duties for our states in life. Seemingly little things can become huge in God's eyes when we offer them to him with love.

Family Prayer

All make the Sign of the Cross.

> *Parent*: Dear Jesus, show us how to love you more! Now let us listen to these words of Saint Thérèse.

A parent or child reads the opening quotation aloud.

> *All*: Blessed Mother Mary, bring us closer to your Son, Jesus.

Saint Thérèse, please pray for us. Amen.

A Story from Saint Thérèse's Life

Thérèse experienced an attack of doubt the night before her profession. Never before had she doubted her vocation. She confided everything to the novice mistress and the mother prioress and was instantly reassured of her vocation. She realized that the devil was tormenting her with an anguish of heart, and as soon as she revealed her doubts, peace filled her heart once again. On September 8, 1890, Thérèse was flooded with peace, joy, and graces as she was professed a Carmelite nun. On September 24, Thérèse received her veil in another ceremony.

Fasting

Today, fast from discouragement and sadness. When tempted to feel downcast, say a prayer and strive to please Jesus.

Almsgiving

Give away your love. Ask the children to write a simple "love" poem or draw a picture; help them with the words. Give it to an unsuspecting family member or friend.

Prayer

> *Today's Intention*: Let's pray for all seminarians, priests, and religious.
>
> *Closing Prayer*: Dear Lord Jesus, help us enter more deeply into the Holy Triduum.
>
> *All pray the Our Father, Hail Mary, and Glory Be.*
>
> *All through the Day*: I want to show my love to Jesus.

GOOD FRIDAY

O Mary, deign to grant the wishes of your poor lamb. During the night of this life, hide her under your mantle.

—*The Poetry of Saint Thérèse of Lisieux*

Parent Reflection

Today is a commemoration of the cornerstone of our Faith. Jesus was brutally tormented, suffered, and died on a cross for us—but not without profound meaning and fruitfulness. This day is central to our lives as Catholics. Structure your day in a manner that is pleasing to God, allowing time to pray and go to services at your parish if possible. Take the time to make this your most deeply prayerful Good Friday ever.

In Saint Thérèse's words above, we can grasp her heartfelt trust in Mother Mary and childlike simplicity in running to a mother in times of need. Ponder what that means in your life right now. What struggles might you surrender? Mother Mary, who stood faithfully at the foot of her Son's Cross, will shelter us all under her mantle, close to her Immaculate Heart. We will grow in holiness when we run to her.

Family Prayer

All make the Sign of the Cross.

> *Parent*: Dear Jesus, help us to truly understand the importance of this day. Now let us listen to these words of Saint Thérèse.

A parent or child reads the opening quotation aloud.

> *All*: Blessed Mother Mary, bring us closer to your Son, Jesus.

Saint Thérèse, please pray for us. Amen.

A Story from Saint Thérèse's Life

Life in the convent for Thérèse was a mix of joy and labor wrapped in the peace of Christ. Thérèse continued to grow in holiness, showering love upon her fellow sisters and offering many prayers and sacrifices for the salvation of souls. Thérèse felt that Jesus was intimately guiding her soul. She yearned to travel the world to be a missionary for God, but she accepted her role, staying put in the convent, saving souls through her humble and loving acts of service and prayer.

Fasting

Follow the fasting rules for Good Friday (see the introduction to this book) but also ask the children to look at a crucifix and thank Jesus for his love.

Almsgiving

Prayerfully consider some act of mercy or charity you can do as a family for someone you know who needs help.

Prayer

Today's Intention: Let us pray for all those who have lost their faith.

Closing Prayer: Dear Lord Jesus, open our hearts to your great love.

All pray the Our Father, Hail Mary, and Glory Be.

All through the Day: Jesus loves us!

HOLY SATURDAY

My mission to make God loved will begin after my death.
I will spend my heaven doing good on earth. I will let fall a
shower of roses.

—Story of a Soul

Parent Reflection

Holy Saturday is a peculiar day; it's a special day, yet it seems so empty. The church appears barren, having been stripped of everything familiar. We may feel a bit lonely and sad. After all, if we are entering into this Holy Triduum through prayer, we can't help but feel the loss of Jesus, much like the disciples felt after losing their Messiah. After his crucifixion, they hid in the upper room with the Blessed Mother, praying deeply for the Holy Spirit to come as Jesus promised and bring them strength and peace. As we wait and pray in the silence of Holy Saturday, we know that Jesus will rise again as he promised. Our hearts can sense peace amid the darkness.

We can glean from Saint Thérèse's words above her great hope in the Resurrection. She was not content with merely saving souls while living on earth but wanted to toil in eternity too! Let us pray that she will shower roses upon us and that we too can desire to save souls here and in eternity.

Family Prayer

All make the Sign of the Cross.

> *Parent*: Dear Jesus, thank you for Saint Thérèse. Let her words of wisdom inspire our hearts to follow your holy will. Now let us listen to these words of Saint Thérèse.

A parent or child reads the opening quotation aloud.

> *All*: Blessed Mother Mary, bring us closer to your Son, Jesus.

> Saint Thérèse, please pray for us. Amen.

A Story from Saint Thérèse's Life

As Jesus guided Thérèse in the virtues, she learned much about practicing charity toward others. Thérèse decided to shower charity on a fellow nun who had caused her discomfort. Instead of avoiding the nun, every time Thérèse encountered the nun, she would give her a tender smile. Finally, the nun asked Thérèse one day why she smiled at her so much. Thérèse explained that she was happy to be in her presence. The loving gestures from Thérèse helped soften the nun's heart.

Fasting

Today, fast from avoiding uncomfortable situations. Try to encounter them with love.

Almsgiving

Give away tender smiles and endeavor to make others feel better.

Prayer

Today's Intention: Let us pray for all world leaders.

Closing Prayer: Dear Lord Jesus, strengthen us in the virtues.

All pray the Our Father, Hail Mary, and Glory Be.

All through the Day: Jesus wants me to be loving always.

EASTER SUNDAY

Parent Reflection

Happy Easter! Christ the Lord is risen today. Alleluia! What a feast this day is—a day of profound celebration! Jesus' rising from the dead has given us the promise of new life, in this life and in the next. Enjoy this feast of all feasts, celebrate fully with your family, and bask in the joy of Easter! Be blessed at Mass and at home with the family. Let the joy of the day fill your heart to overflowing, carrying it with you in the days ahead, being a beacon of light for others. Alleluia!

Family Prayer

All make the Sign of the Cross.

> *Parent*: Dear Jesus, thank you for your incredible love for us and the gift of your Church! Now let us listen to these words of Saint Thérèse.

A parent or child reads the opening quotation aloud.

> *All*: Blessed Mother Mary, bring us closer to your Son, Jesus.
>
> Saint Thérèse, please pray for us. Amen.

A Story from Saint Thérèse's Life

One day, Thérèse was pondering her vocation. She thought about the vocations of others—of apostles, martyrs, crusaders, missionaries, priests, saints, prophets, doctors, and more. She expressed to Jesus in prayer that she wanted to preach the Gospel on all five continents, but she felt "little" and "powerless." Thérèse opened her bible and read the First Epistle to the Corinthians. She scanned through the passage about the wide-ranging gifts given to various people. Thérèse discovered peace in these words, which shouted up from the page to pierce her heart. She understood that it was love alone that caused Christ's members to act. Without love, apostles could not preach— love comprised all vocations. Charity was indeed Thérèse's vocation. She wholeheartedly embraced her calling and exuberantly cried out her *fiat* to God (expressed in the opening quotation for this day).

Fasting and Almsgiving

Because it is Easter, the culmination of the penitential season of Lent, it is obviously not a day of fasting and almsgiving. Even so, encourage your family to retain the spirit of prayer fostered in their hearts throughout the season. Ask the family to remember to offer up little sacrifices and sufferings every day and to continually reach out to others around them. God is very pleased with our little acts of love.

Prayer

Today's Intention: Let us pray for the Church.

Closing Prayer: Dear Lord Jesus, let us be your love to others.

All pray the Our Father, Hail Mary, and Glory Be.

All through the Day: Jesus Christ is risen today!

Endeavor to remember Saint Thérèse's spiritual childhood. Keep in mind her words: "Jesus does not demand great actions from us but simply surrender and gratitude" (*Story of a Soul*, 188).

NOVENA PRAYER TO SAINT THÉRÈSE

O Glorious Saint Thérèse, whom Almighty God has raised up to aid and inspire the human family, I implore your miraculous intercession. You are so powerful in obtaining every need of body and spirit from the Heart of God. Holy Mother Church proclaims you "Prodigy of Miracles . . . the Greatest Saint of Modern Times." Now I fervently beseech you to answer my petition (*mention it here*) and to carry out your promises of spending heaven doing good on earth . . . of letting fall from heaven a shower of roses. Little Flower, give me your childlike faith, to see the Face of God in the people and experiences of my life, and to love God with full confidence. Saint Thérèse, my Carmelite sister, I will fulfill your plea "to be made known everywhere," and I will continue to lead others to Jesus through you. Amen.

PRAYER BEFORE A CRUCIFIX

Look down upon me, good and gentle Jesus,

while before your face I humbly kneel and,

with burning soul,

pray and beseech you

to fix deep in my heart lively sentiments

of faith, hope, and charity;

true contrition for my sins;

and a firm purpose of amendment.

While I contemplate,

with great love and tender pity,

your five most precious wounds,

pondering over them within me

and calling to mind the words which David,

your prophet, said of you, my Jesus:

"They have pierced My hands and My feet,

they have numbered all My bones" (Ps 21:17–18).

Amen.

On the Fridays of Lent, the faithful receive a plenary indulgence if they recite the prayer before a crucifix. The indulgence is a partial indulgence any other time.

Pray these prayers for the Holy Father's intentions: Our Father, Hail Mary, and Glory Be.

BIBLIOGRAPHY

Letters of Saint Thérèse. Vol. 1. Translated by John Clarke, O.C.D. Washington, DC: Institute of Carmelite Studies Publications, 1982.

The Poetry of Saint Thérèse of Lisieux. Translated by Donald Kinney, O.C.D. Washington, DC: Institute of Carmelite Studies Publications, 1995.

The Prayers of Saint Thérèse of Lisieux, Doctor of the Church. Translated by Aletheia Kane, O.C.D. Washington, DC: Institute of Carmelite Studies Publications, 1995.

Story of a Soul. 3rd ed. Translated from the original manuscripts by John Clarke, O.C.D. Washington, DC: Institute of Carmelite Studies Publications, 1995.

NOTES

1. Pope Benedict XVI's Homily at Ash Wednesday Mass (*Zenit*, February 13, 2013), http://www.zenit.org/en/articles/benedict-xvi-s-homily-at-ash-wednesday-mass.

2. Ida Friederike Goerres, *The Hidden Face: A Study of St. Thérèse of Lisieux* (San Francisco: Ignatius Press, 2003), 66.

3. Vincent J. O'Malley, *Ordinary Suffering of Extraordinary Saints* (Huntington, IN: Our Sunday Visitor, 1999), 38.

Donna-Marie Cooper O'Boyle is an award-winning author and journalist, speaker, reviewer, and the EWTN television host of *Everyday Blessings for Catholic Moms*, which she created. A Catholic wife and mother of five, Cooper O'Boyle was noted as one of the Top Ten Most Fascinating Catholics in 2009 by *Faith & Family Live*. She enjoyed a decade-long friendship with Blessed Mother Teresa of Calcutta and became a Lay Missionary of Charity. For many years her spiritual director was Servant of God John A. Hardon, S.J., who also served as one of Mother Teresa's spiritual directors.

Cooper O'Boyle was invited by the Holy See in 2008 to participate in an international congress for women at the Vatican to mark the twentieth anniversary of the apostolic letter *Mulieris Dignitatem* (*On the Dignity and Vocation of Women*). She received apostolic blessings from Pope John Paul II and Pope Benedict XVI on her books and work and a special blessing from Pope John Paul II for her work with Blessed Mother Teresa. Cooper O'Boyle is the author of several books on faith and family, including *Bringing Lent Home with Mother Teresa*, *Mother Teresa and Me*, *Embracing Motherhood*, and *The Domestic Church*. She has been featured by Zenit news and *Rome Reports*, and is a frequent guest on EWTN's *Bookmark*, *Faith & Culture*, and *Vatican Insider*.